Nine Little Flags

by Joaquin Garcia
illustrated by Diane Paterson

Practice Decodable 52

McGraw Hill Education

Bothell, WA • Chicago, IL • Columbus, OH • New York, NY

MHEonline.com

Send all inquiries to:
McGraw-Hill Education
8787 Orion Place
Columbus, OH 43240

ISBN: 978-0-02-135455-9
MHID: 0-02-135455-3

Printed in China

8 9 10 11 12 DSS 27 26 25 24 23

The kids liked to walk. Surprise!
Little flags were in a yard!

"Nine little flags!" smiled Iris.
"Will squirrels on bikes zigzag past?"

Big Mike smiled.

"Well, we must dig a wide ditch."

"We must not hit the pipes and wires."

"This is a map of pipes and wires.
Flags help us miss wires and pipes."

"And squirrels can't ride bikes.
They ride on skates!" kidded Mike.